The Calligraphy Work Book

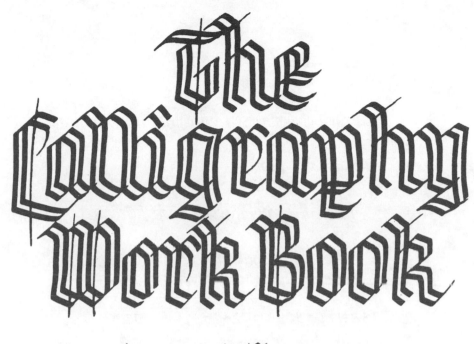

The Calligraphy Work Book

George E. Thomson

Sterling Publishing Co., Inc.   New York

Library of Congress Cataloging-in-Publication Data

Thomson, George Lawrie

The calligraphy work book / George L. Thomson.
    p.   cm.
  "First published in 1985 in the U.K. by
Thorsons Publishing Group."

ISBN 0-8069-7262-9   paper

  1. Calligraphy   I. Title
Z43. T478   1985   89-29696
745.6' 1977--dc20   CIP

10   9   8   7   6   5   4   3   2   1

Contents

Introduction

The four alphabets presented here are designed to be examples typical of specific FAMILIES of scripts, but also legible and easy to learn and write. They have been modified where necessary to make certain letters intelligible to modern eyes.

The Black Letter capitals particularly have been rationalised and made recognisable. While we agree that the various versions of capitals in many Gothic scripts can be beautiful examples of abstract decoration, no one today would claim that they are LEGIBLE.

For anyone who would wish to go on eventually to write the more exotic black letter scripts, the mastery of the very simple version here shown will provide a working knowledge of the disciplines required. Though it may look quite complicated to the layman, the letters need no more strokes than any other script.

Those who are interested in RUSTIC script may wonder why it is not included here. In our opinion, it is one of the worst scripts ever invented - illegible, badly proportioned, uneven in colour owing to the exaggerated pen angle. It may be that it looks so inept even when written by a master scribe that the efforts of a beginner can be a near approximation, thus giving him a false estimation of his own abilities. Admittedly it is historically important, so leave it to the paleographers!

The Round Hand version given here is of the same family as Carolingian, Humanistic and Edward Johnston's Foundational Hand. Again, to simplify things for the learner, where there are alternative forms of particular letters, we have chosen only one. It is a simple matter to change to a preferred form AFTER the script is mastered. These remarks also apply to the Italic script recommended here. Note here that ascenders and descenders may be made as long as the scribe wishes, providing the space between the lines is proportionately increased. Bear in mind, however, that the longer they become, the more difficult it is to keep them of even length and slant. Slight discrepancies which would not be noticed in normal writing will be glaringly obvious on letters of exaggerated length.

We have emphasised the necessity of keeping the same angle of the pen's chisel edge. PEN ANGLE is invariable in the best scripts. Changing the angle at every stroke means pivoting the whole hand, and would result in an unacceptably slow writing speed. Even a master calligrapher would find it impossible to write fast enough to keep the "flow" of the writing.

Some black letter scripts have square bases to the upright strokes of the letters, but we do not recommend this to any but the most advanced students. These should keep the pen angle constant to the foot of the stroke, ▮ ◣ filling in the square base or slight serif with the left corner of the nib point. Changing the angle to finish horizontally, besides being fiendishly difficult, results in a clumsy, heavy looking letter, the vertical strokes shading from narrow to thick.

While it may be agreed that these four scripts are representative of the main families of scripts, some may wonder why there is no mention of Trajan Roman, the ancestor of all. The answer is that here we are dealing purely with pen-formed characters, and it is generally accepted that Classic Roman capitals were drawn with the brush. For those interested, there are some excellent books dealing solely with Roman lettering.

A word about the spacing of letters. This cannot be done mechanically. There should be an optical balance of the area of space on each side of a letter. To assess your own spacing, look at each group of three letters in the word, and it will be obvious when one pair of letters appears either cramped or too far apart.

As a general rule, O's should be close to each other, OI slightly further apart,

and 11 further still. The diagram
below illustrates what we mean.

VOOIIAV

While this applies to all lettering, it
is most important in words written in
capitals only. For the best results,
always do a preliminary rough layout.

Four Easy Scripts

The student calligrapher will find here
the four main scripts from which all the
others are derived ; uncial, round hand,
black letter and italic.

Each one is reduced to the simplest possible
forms, with a few modifications here and
there to bring them into line with modern
usage.

These basic shapes can be built upon as a
completely reliable base as the student
progresses, perhaps to study under a
professional scribe; but they can stand
on their own merits for busy people who

simply want an easily written script
for occasional use.

The minimum of equipment required is:
ink, pens, paper, a board, T-square and
set-squares, and compasses and dividers.
Few crafts need less working tools.

The cheapest ink you can get will serve
while you are practising, but for finished
work you must have a good black ink.
This may be waterproof or non-waterproof.
For coloured lettering, use diluted poster
colour rather than inks.

William Mitchell's Pedigree Round Hand
Pens can be bought as a set, with a holder,
on a card. Osmiroid and Platignum
make useful fountain pen lettering sets.
For very large lettering you may
eventually want to buy witch or poster

pens. It is not too difficult to make your own pens from twigs or bamboo.

Any smooth white paper will do for practice, but for better work, get something more substantial. Notices and labels will quite often require stiff card.

Any board big enough to hold your paper will do. It should be propped up at an angle. Professional scribes may prefer an angle of 45° or so, but you will probably be more comfortable with something less steep.

Use the T-square and set-squares to line off your paper, measuring the height of your lettering in pen-widths. Hold the pen sideways. The height will vary according to the size of the nib you are using.

Pin one or two sheets of paper on the board, big enough to cover it. This provides a resilient backing for the writing sheet, and makes for more comfortable writing.

Fold a piece of paper about 6" wide and pin across the board about two thirds of the way up. Your writing sheet goes under this, and is held without pinning, so that it can be moved up, a line at a time, to the proper height. This also helps to keep it clean.

Your pen may be dipped in the ink for practice work, but keep a cloth handy to wipe the back of the nib. For really fine writing, fill the nib from the front with a brush, so that no ink gets on the back at all. This is necessary to preserve the sharpness of the thin strokes.

Do not practise for so long that you become

bored. Stop! because then you can go on repeating a mistake without noticing it. Calligraphy should be enjoyable, and should look as though it had been done with pleasure.

When you can write a script passably, look for opportunities to USE it. Find someone who needs a poster, a notice, even a label, and do it without charge. You may not be satisfied with your layout or writing, but the chance to do a real job is of great value, and the more experience you get, the more confidence you will have.

If you can achieve complete command of these four scripts, you will be well on the way to becoming the Complete Calligrapher.

But you will never arrive! The more aware you become of perfection, the less likely it seems of achievement. And this is the charm of genuine calligraphy. Even the very best has little flaws and imperfections to remind us that the most polished and assured scribe is still only human, and that this was the work of a fallible human hand. If you want every letter to be identical every time, then you must turn to the machine, to the printing press, or to the typewriter. But that way you can never feel the inner glow of pride and satisfaction which comes from the completion of a not quite perfect piece of lettering which is all your own from start to finish.

Before using a broad pen for the first time, teach your hand the rhythms of broad pen writing by practising the three movements shown in the diagram overleaf.

Cut a piece of stiff card to represent the pen made large, and hold it by the sides so that the chisel edge tip lies flat on the paper. Follow each stroke in proper order, but the very first rule is that the EDGE must always remain parallel with the dotted lines, no matter whether the direction of the stroke is a curve or a straight line.

Use as little pressure as possible. The card tip, and the pen tip when you come to use it, should only touch the paper. It should glide over the surface, not plough into it.

Each script has a preliminary practice diagram which incorporates all the strokes used in that script.

The drawing shows the relaxed pen grip. Never hold the pen tightly, with the fist clenched. The angle shown is an approximation. Experiment until you find one which allows you to follow the diagrams without strain. The pen edge itself will guide you; if it runs smoothly, you are doing it right, if it digs in or skids, you are doing it wrong.

To start with, it is best to move the pen quite slowly, but as your hand becomes accustomed to the new rules, you will write with confidence and more quickly.

For the sake of simplicity, only one form of letter is shown in each script, though there are many variations.

Cut a piece of stiff card this width to represent the pen

Practise these three strokes until you can keep the pen tip always parallel with the dotted red lines

Only four rules need be memorised

Keep your letters even in size. Keep the vertical letters upright, never slanting backwards. [In the case of italic, keep an even slant forwards.] Always have enough space between lines to prevent tangling of tops and tails. And finally, leave ample margins around the edges of each page.

Now you can start on the script of your choice, beginning with practice on the preliminary diagram.

Then, using your card strip, go over each letter in turn. Repeat each letter until you can write it automatically without having to check the order and starting place of each stroke.

Next, go over the small letters at the top of

the page in the same way, using a dry
pen of the appropriate size. Keep your
touch very light.

As soon as you have confidence, write with
ink in your pen, copying under the
small letters. Use a separate sheet of
paper if you do not wish to write on the
book itself.

Now try putting together words and sentences,
keeping your letters closely spaced and even,
leaving the space of an "o" between each
word.

Each of the four scripts is what is known as
a FORMAL script, but the italic can
develop into an everyday cursive hand
if it is written rapidly, with ligatures.
In a formal script, the letters are not
joined together.

At the end of each section is a selection of
examples, illustrating some of the
ways each script may be put to use.

The scripts are in chronological order.
UNCIAL came from the Roman capital
letter. ROUND HAND or Carolingian
came later, and then BLACK LETTER
a compressed book hand. Last is
ITALIC, which is also a compressed
book hand, but much lighter and
containing a more cursive element.

Formal scripts should be written with some
care, but remember they can also be
written fairly rapidly, because they were
used for writing books before the invention
of the printing press. Any scribe who took
years to write and illuminate a single text
[as the old myth claims,] would very quickly

have found himself out of a job.

The beginner's two main difficulties are likely
to be, keeping the long strokes straight
and vertical [it is very easy to introduce
a backward slant], and keeping the
letters the same height throughout.
But never despair. As time goes by, the
things you found difficult will become
easy.

practise, practise, practise!

But now, you may be thinking, does
one make the thin vertical line? No,
not with a pointed pen. It is made by
turning the pen edge and sliding it sideways,
like the runner of a sledge.
Use it as a decorative "grace note" to embellish
capital letters only, never on minuscules –
[small letters.] Note the spelling, because
too many people are now using MINI-scule,
probably influenced by minicar and miniskirt!

uncial

Practise pen handling with the dummy
pen point before you attempt the letters.
Most letters can be written with only one
or two of the strokes in the diagram.
These large sweeping movements help to fix
the right movements and sequences in the
mind, and re-educate the writing muscles.
Use a light touch to counter the "death grip"
used by so many – the cause of writers' cramp.
It is most important to keep the writing edge
of your pen in contact with the paper all along
its width, AND at the same angle as the
dotted lines, no matter whether you are
making straight or curved lines. Beginners
often turn the wrist and the pen edge to follow
a curve. Resist the temptation to do this!

20

PRACTICE
DIAGRAM

a a a a a a a b b b b b

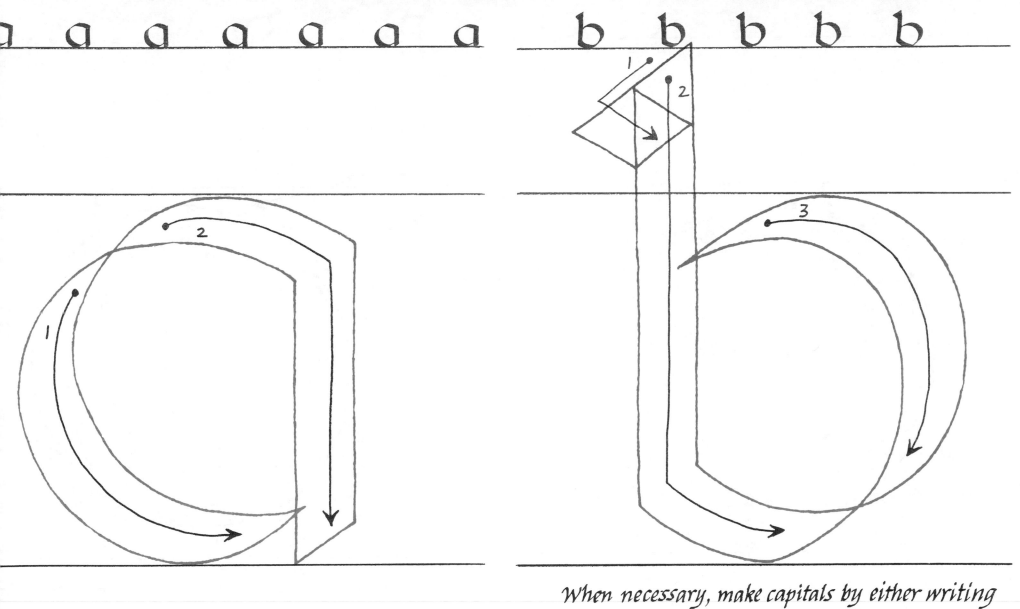

When necessary, make capitals by either writing
the letter bigger or by changing the colour

21

22

e e e e e e e e   f f f f f f f

24

l l l l l l l m m m m m m

n n n n n n   o o o o o o

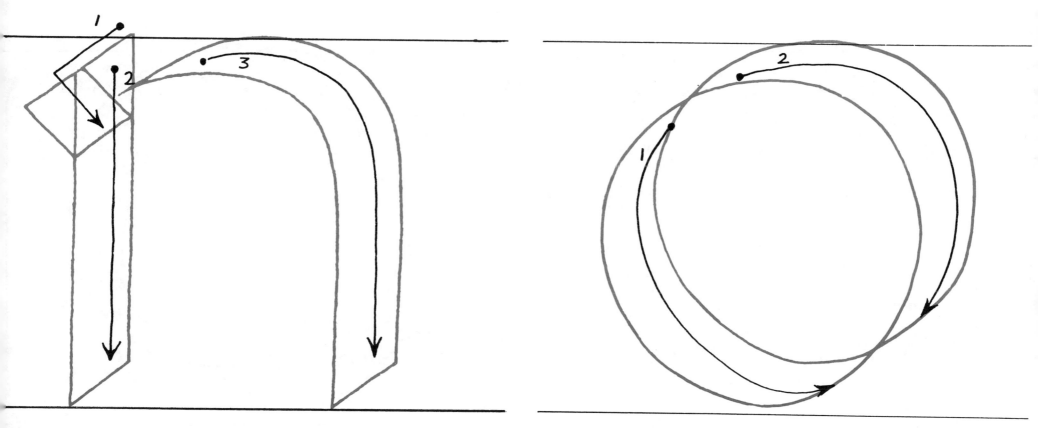

p p p p p p p   Q Q Q Q Q Q Q

R R R R R R R

S S S S S S

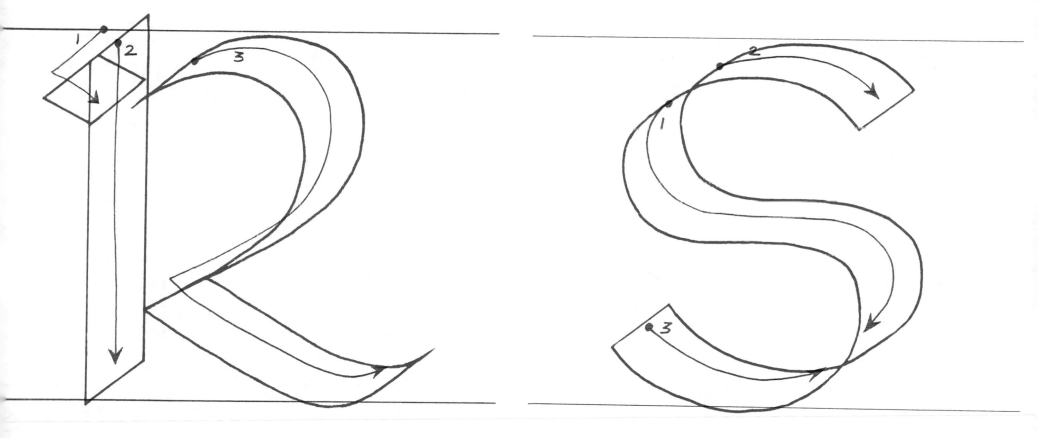

τ τ τ τ τ τ τ   υ υ υ υ υ υ

Change angle to make this stroke wider

12 12 12 12 12 12   3 3 3 3 3 3

4 4 4 4 4 4

5 5 5 5 5 5

8 8 8 8 8 8 9 9 9 9 9 9 9

CELTIC ART

a series of lectures by Professor M.P. Smythe

·

in Carnegie Hall
7 pm Fridays

❖

entrance free

Lub am faillean nuair a tha e maoth

(Bend the sapling while it is young [Gaelic])

mackie

farrel

linsey

weasel

basketry

biscuits

gallery

Name plates may be enlarged to any size you wish

Ticket labels can be written on thin smooth card

round hand

Practise pen handling with the dummy
pen point before you attempt the letters.
Most letters can be written with only one
or two of the strokes in the diagram.
These large sweeping movements help to fix
the right movements and sequences in the
mind, and re-educate the writing muscles.
Use a light touch to counter the "death grip"
used by so many - the cause of writers' cramp.
It is most important to keep the writing edge
of your pen in contact with the paper all along
its width, AND at the same angle as the
dotted lines, no matter whether you are
making straight or curved lines. Beginners
often turn the wrist and the pen edge to follow
a curve. Resist the temptation to do this!

44

Keep the pen slant the same, whether you are
doing vertical, horizontal or curved strokes

a a a a a a a b b b b b b

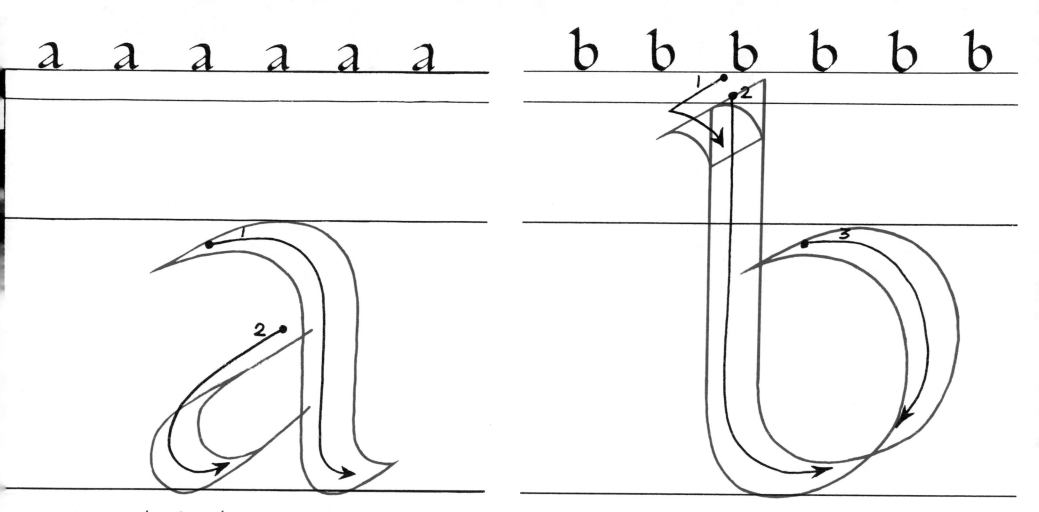

Whatever size of pen is used, small letters are
4½ penwidths high, capitals 6½, and tops
and tails 2½ above and below.

c c c c c c c   d d d d d d

46

e e e e e e   f f f f f f

g g g g g g h h h h h

ij   ij   ij   ij   ij   ij   k   k   k   k

l l l   l l l   m m m m m m

n n n n n n   o o o o o o

p p p p p   a a a a a a

r r r r r r r   s s s s s s

t t t t t t u u u u u u

Z Z Z Z Z Z   A A   A A

F F F F F   G G G G G G

H H H H H H   IJ IJ IJ IJ IJ

K K K K K K K   l l l l l l l

MMMMMMM NNNNNN

O O O O O p p p p p

Q Q Q Q Q Q Q   R R R R R

u u u u u u   v v v v v

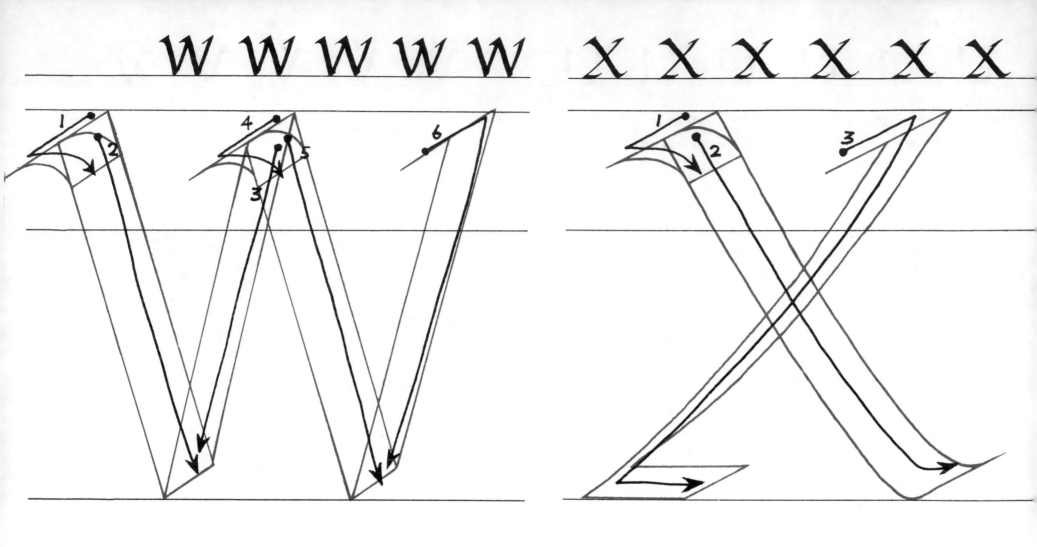

Y Y Y Y Y Y   Z Z Z Z Z

& & & & &

12 12 12 12 12 12

3 3 3 3 3 3   4 4 4 4 4 4

5 5 5 5 5   6 6 6 6 6 6

7 7 7 7 7 7

8 8 8 8 8

9 9 9 9 9   0 0 0 0 0 0

£ £ £ £ £ £ $ $ $ $ $

spring
sale

cashier

Room 23

club meeting

"ECOLOGY"

speaker James Smith

discussion

coffee

22 May at 7 pm

Always leave a good margin at the bottom

Pater noster

qui es in coelis : sanct-
ificetur nomen tuum.
Adveniat regnum tuum.
Fiat voluntas tua, sicut
in coelo et in terra. Pan-
em nostrum quotidian-
um da nobis hodie. Et
dimitte nobis debita nos-
tra, sicut et nos dimitti-
mus debitoribus nos-
tris. Et ne nos inducas
in tentationem. Sed lib-
era nos a malo. amen

Braemar Bridge

School Orchestra

recital

Bach

Brahms

Beethoven

on March 22 at 5.30 pm

in

the School Hall

✦

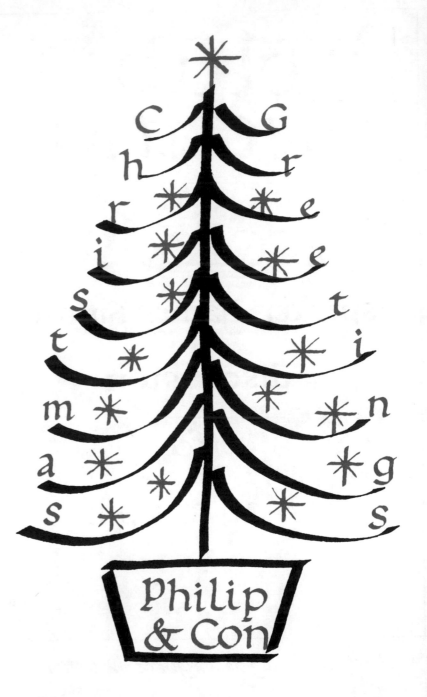

black letter

Practise pen handling with the dummy
pen point before you attempt the letters.
Most letters can be written with only one
or two of the strokes in the diagram.
These large sweeping movements help to fix
the right movements and sequences in the
mind, and re-educate the writing muscles.
Use a light touch to counter the "death grip"
used by so many – the cause of writers' cramp.
It is most important to keep the writing edge
of your pen in contact with the paper all along
its width, AND at the same angle as the
dotted lines, no matter whether you are
making straight or curved lines. Beginners
often turn the wrist and the pen edge to follow
a curve. Resist the temptation to do this!

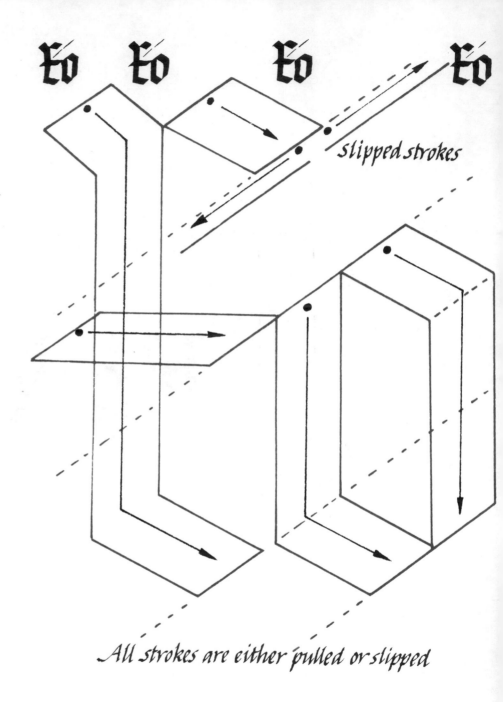

slipped strokes

All strokes are either pulled or slipped

𝖆 𝖆 𝖆 𝖆 𝖆 𝖆 𝖆   𝖇 𝖇 𝖇 𝖇 𝖇

start slightly above the line

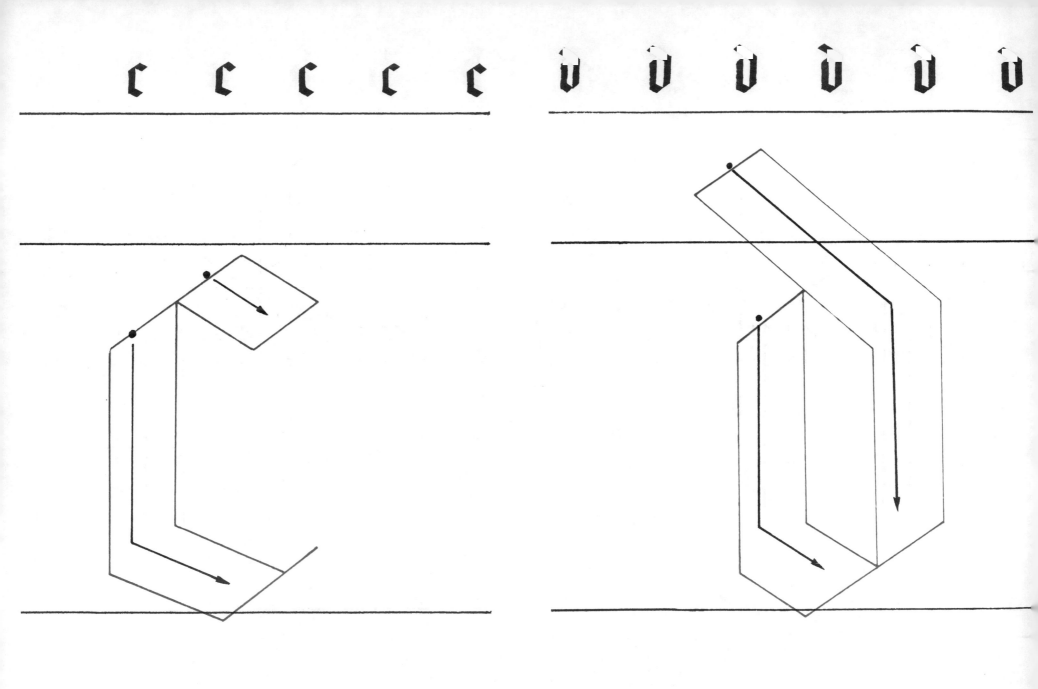

e e e e e e e   f f f f f

g g g g g h h h h h h

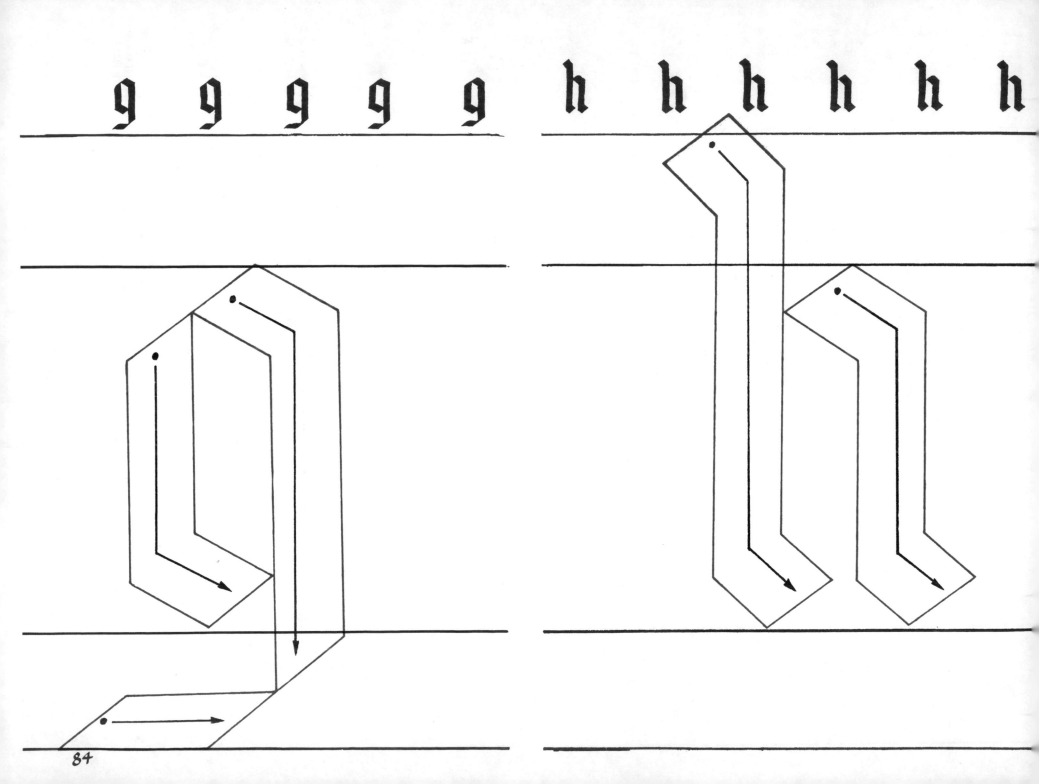

ÿ ÿ ÿ ÿ ÿ ÿ   k k k k k

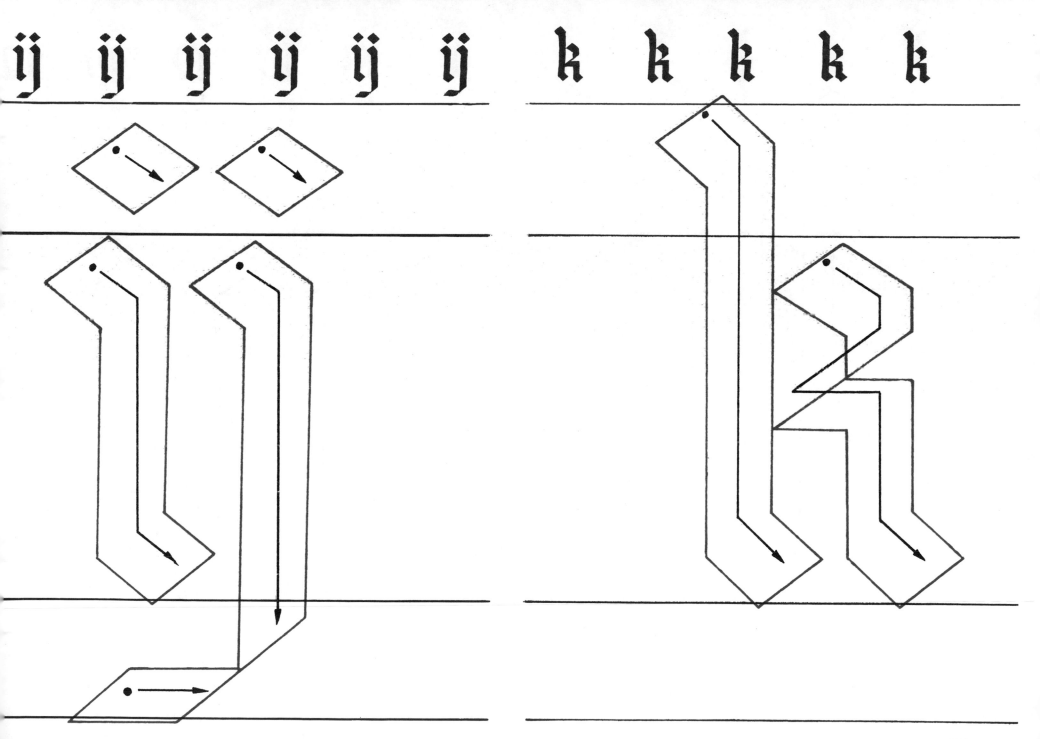

𝔩 𝔩 𝔩 𝔩 𝔩 𝔪 𝔪 𝔪 𝔪 𝔪 𝔪

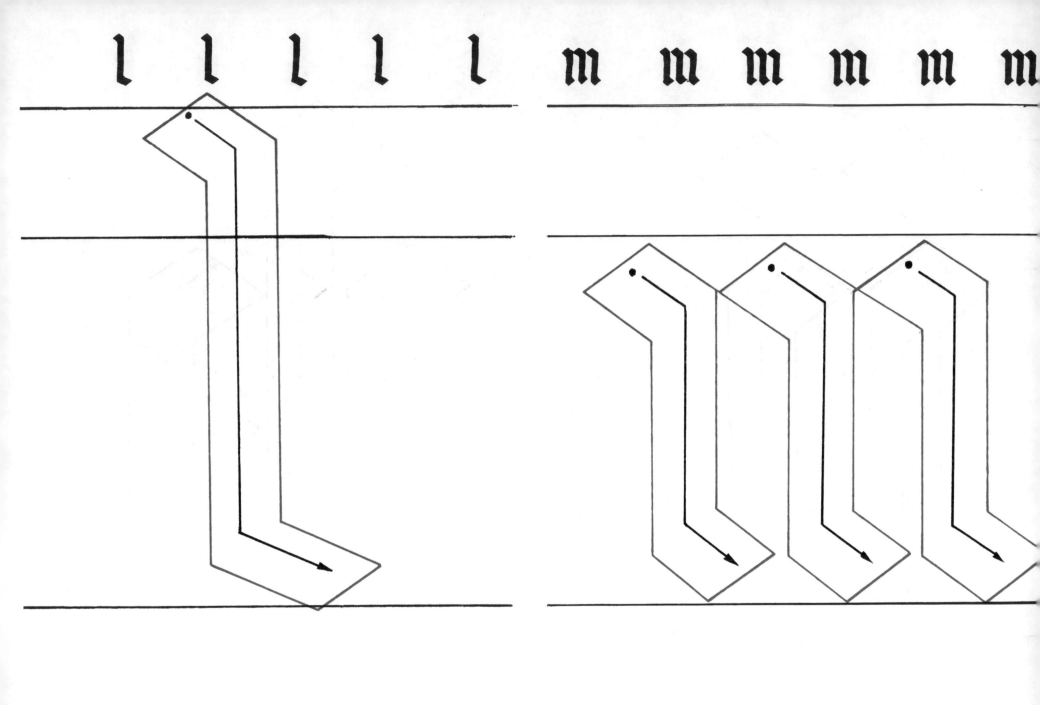

n n n n n n o o o o o o

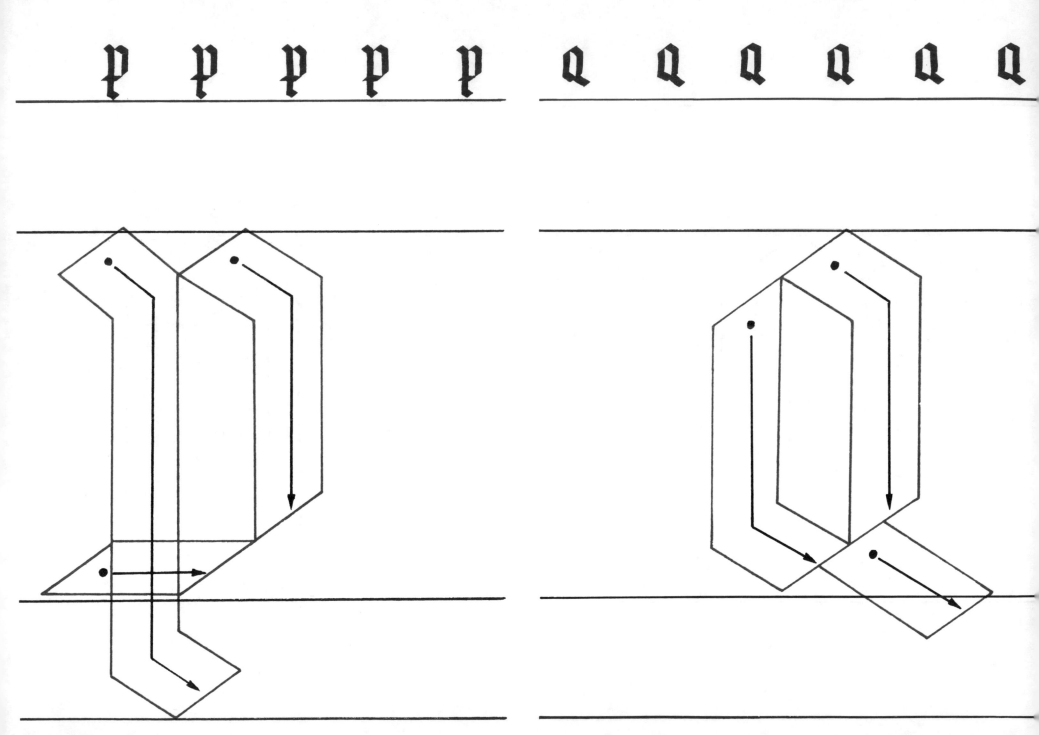

r r r r r r r r   s s s s s s

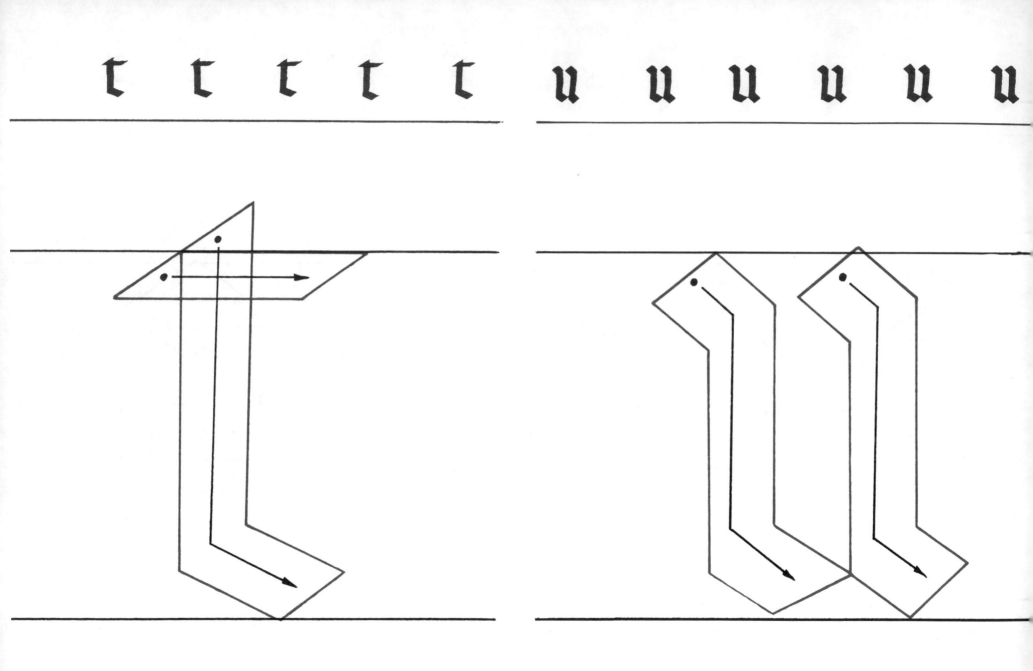

𝔳　𝔳　𝔳　𝔳　𝔳　𝔳　𝔴　𝔴　𝔴　𝔴　𝔴

start slightly above line

Make this line by turning
the pen sideways. This is decorative and may be
omitted, especially in smaller sizes.

95

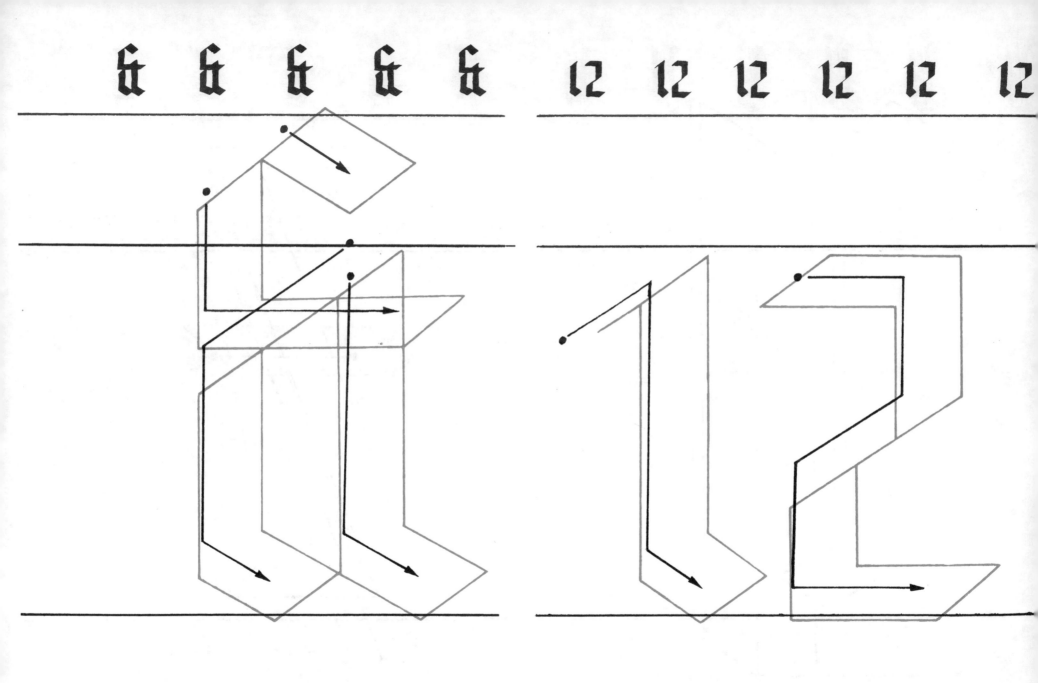

3　　3　　3　　3　　3　　3　　　　4　　4　　4　　4　　4

£$ £$ £$ £$ £$ £$

Certificate
of merit
presented to

John M Smith

on completing a prime course of studies at the Green Valley College

Verdi

Beethoven

Schubert

Boccherini

Tchaikowsky

Bed and
Breakfast

Exit

contributions

Sale

Souvenirs

Contrary to expectations, this is perhaps the easiest to write, as all the lines are straight.

abcdefghijk
lmnopqrstu
vwxyz

To add hair lines, slide your pen sideways

abcdefghijkl

Experiment with different heights, using same pen

mnopqrstuvw
xyz

Better
is a dinner of
herbs
where love is
than a fatted ox
and hatred
with it

Bar

Certificate

Entrance

no admittance

Vacancies

Out

Corot

Rembrandt

Constable

Botticelli

Mantegna

Practise pen handling with the dummy
    pen point before you attempt the letters.
    Most letters can be written with only one
    or two of the strokes in the diagram.
These large sweeping movements help to fix
    the right movements and sequences in the
    mind, and re-educate the writing muscles.
Use a light touch to counter the "death grip"
    used by so many – the cause of writers' cramp.
It is most important to keep the writing edge
    of your pen in contact with the paper all along
    its width, AND at the same angle as the
    dotted lines, no matter whether you are
    making straight or curved lines. Beginners
    often turn the wrist and the pen edge to follow
    a curve. Resist the temptation to do this!

TEST
FIGURE

If your pen slant
is correct, the
upright and the
horizontal strokes
will be the
same width

Whatever size of pen is used, small letters are
5 pen widths high, capitals 6½, and tops and
tails 2½ above and below.

a a a a a a a a a a a

b b b b b b b b

When practising on these large letters, use
the whole arm, and do not move the wrist.

c c c c c c c c c   d d d d d d d d d

e e e e e e e e e e

f f f f f f f

g g g g g g g g g

h h h h h h h h

ij ij ij ij ij ij ij ij ij ij

k k k k k k k

l l l l l l l l

m m m m m m m m

n　*n*　*n*　*n*　*n*　*n*　*n*　*n*　　　*o*　*o*　*o*　*o*　*o*　*o*　*o*

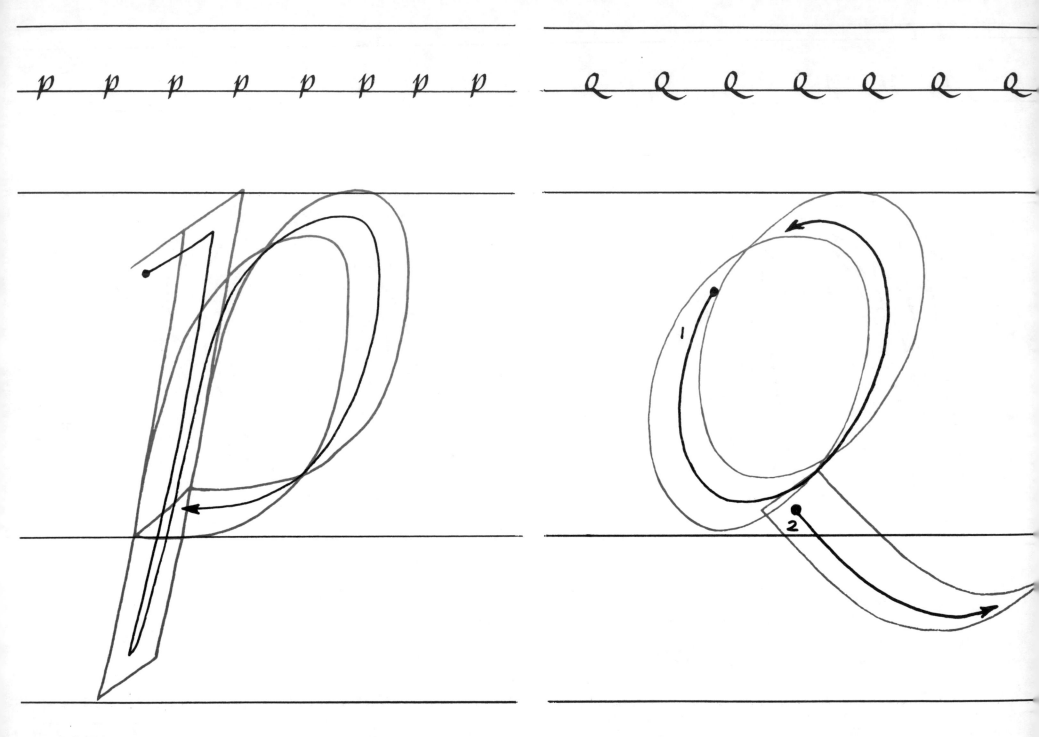

r r r r r r r r   s s s s s s s

t t t t t t t u u u u u u u u

V V V V V V V V V
W W W W W W W

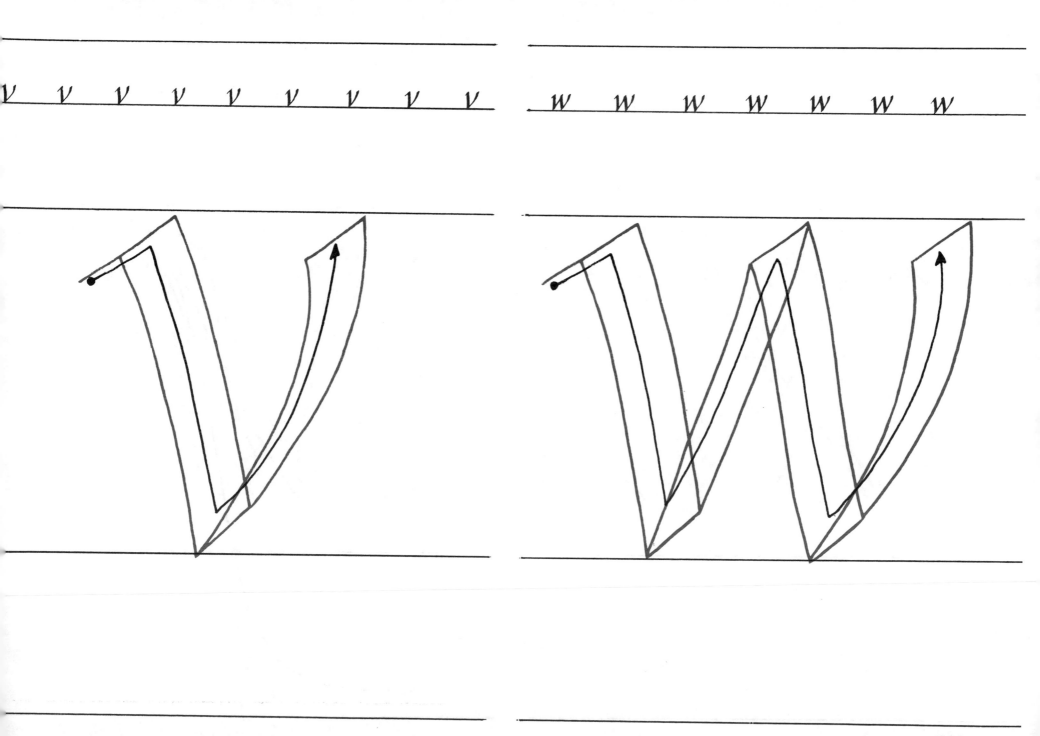

x   *x*   *x*   *x*   *x*   *x*   *x*   *y*   *y*   *y*   *y*   *y*   *y*   *y*   *y*

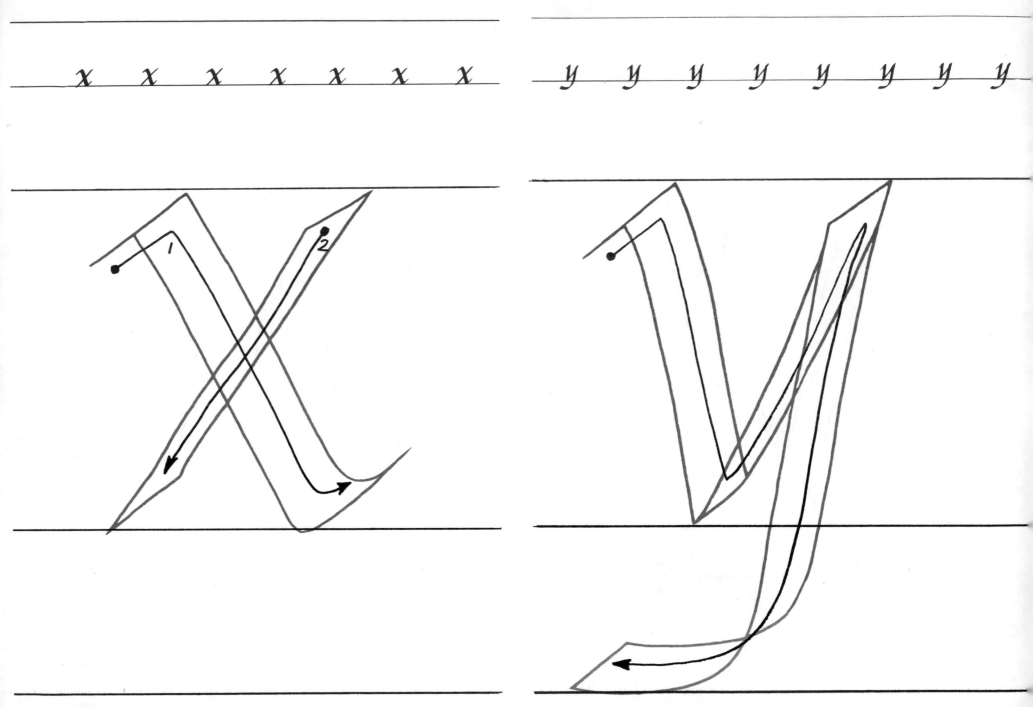

z z z z z z z z

A A A A A A A

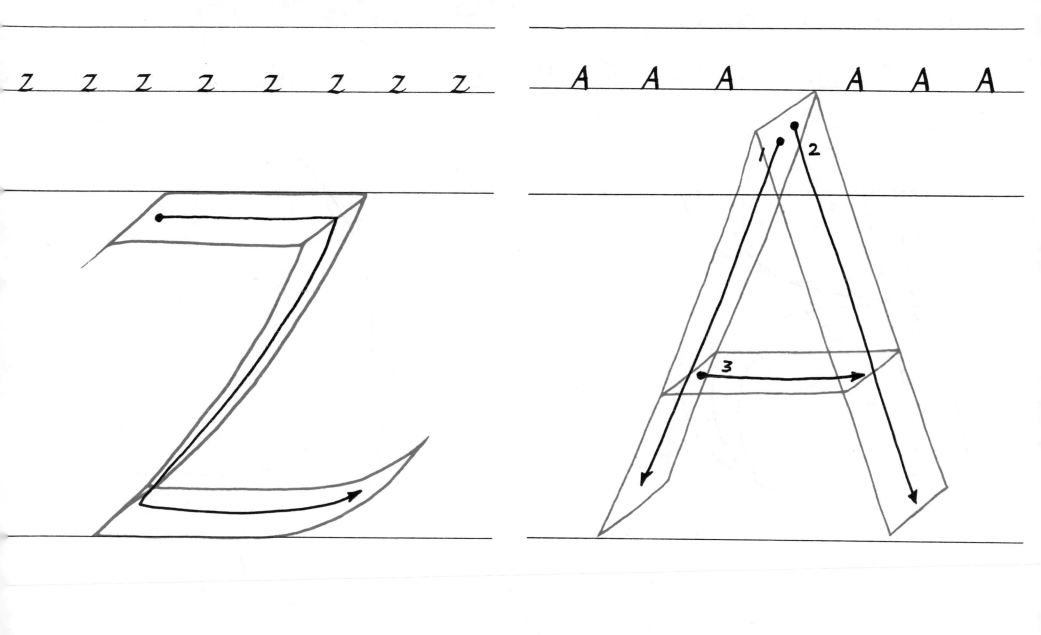

B B B B B B B   C C C C C C C C

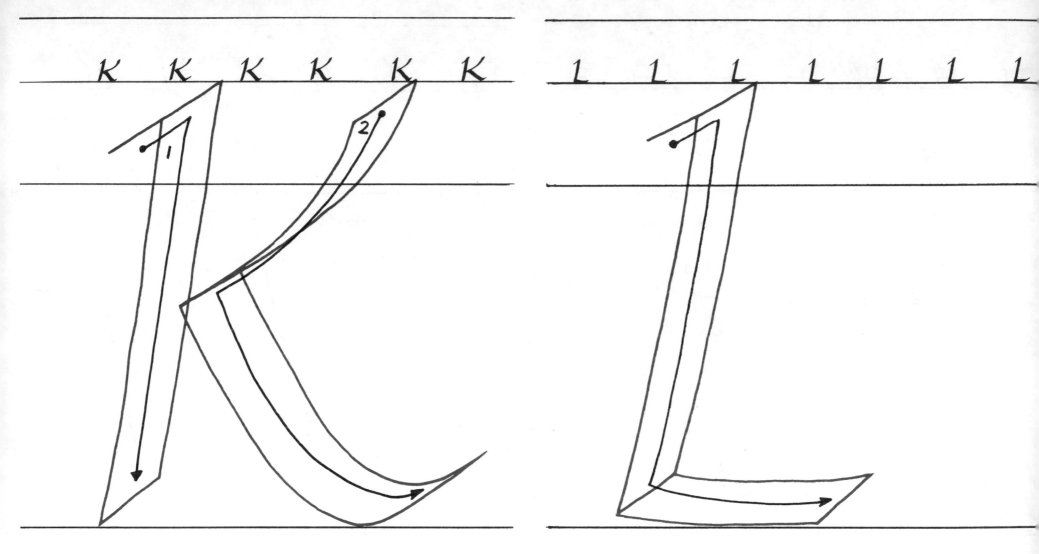

M M M M M M M   N N N N N

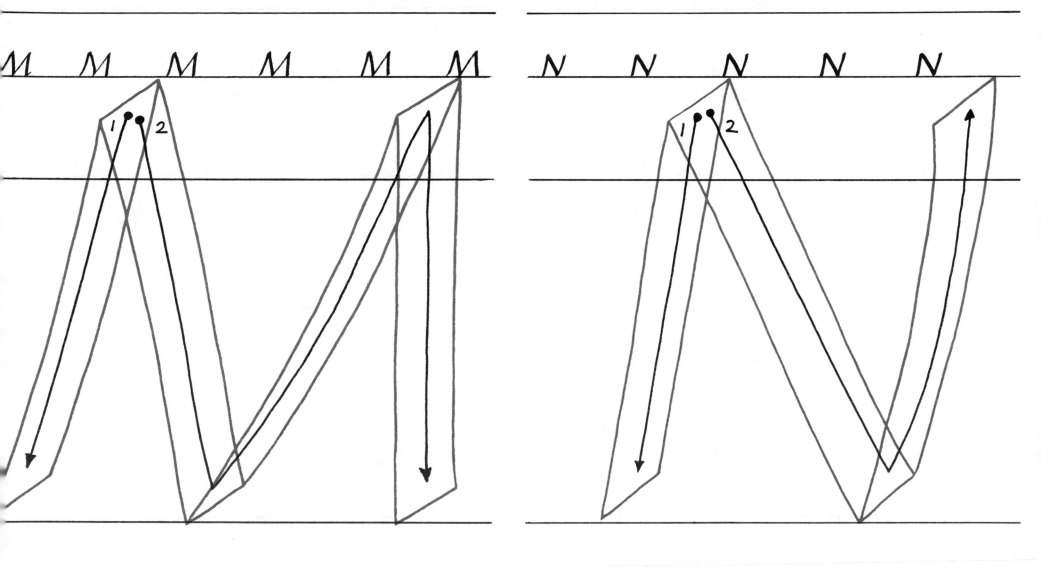

O   O   O   O   O   O   O

P   P   P   P   P   P   P

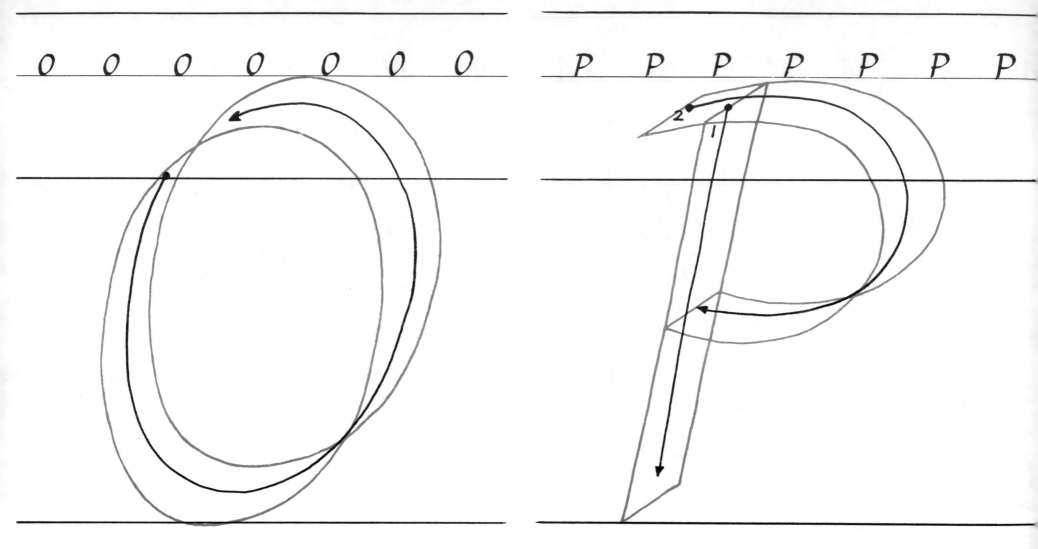

Q Q Q Q Q Q Q Q Q Q Q R R R R R R R

S S S S S S S   T T T T T T T T

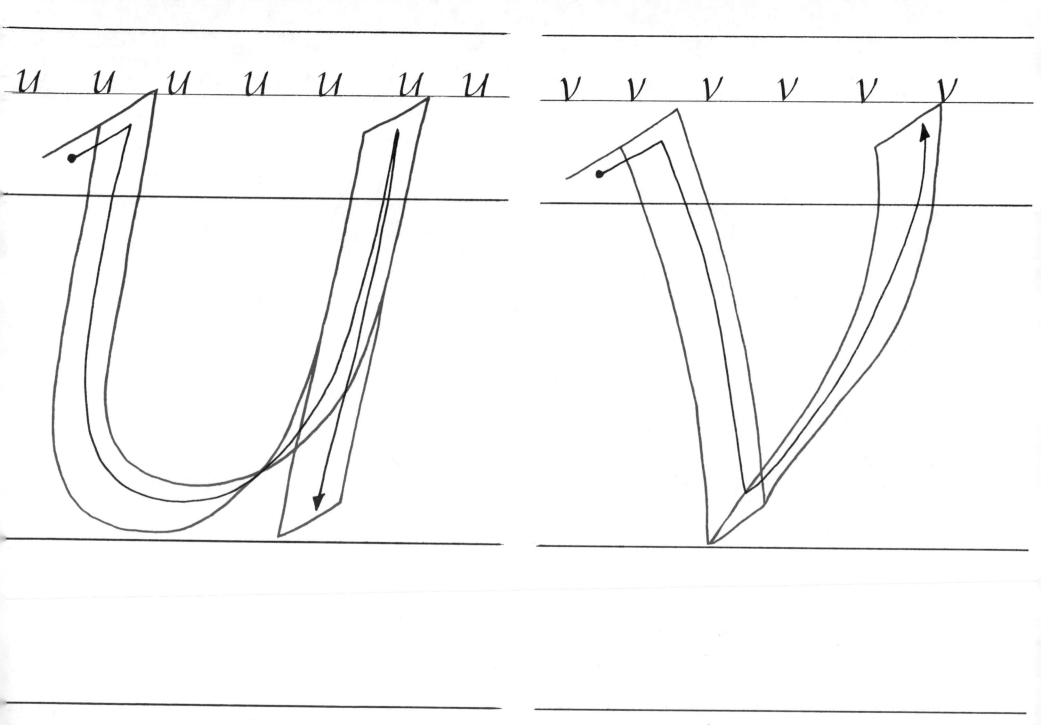

U U U U U U U

V V V V V V V

W   W   W   W   W   W   x   x   x   x   x   x

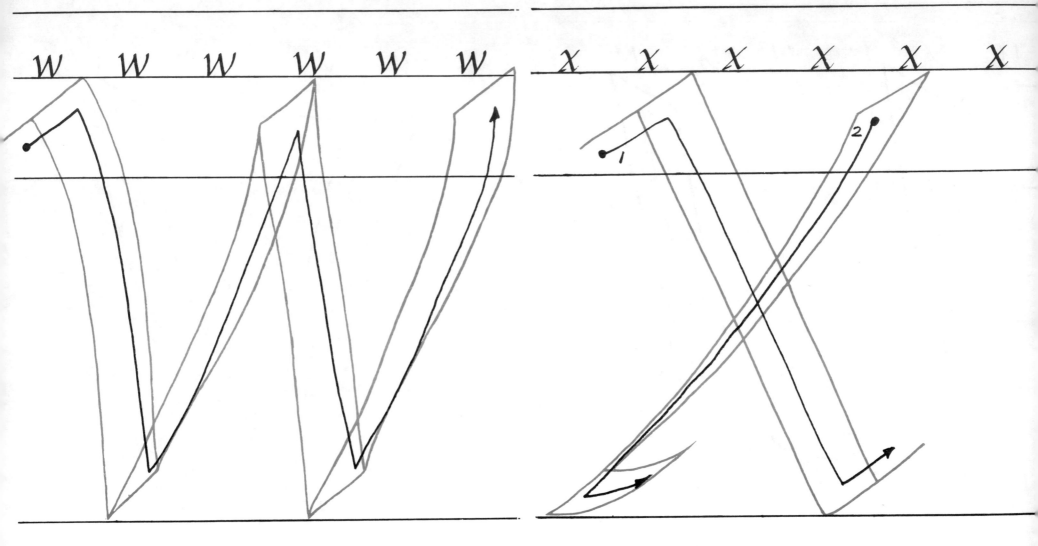

y y y y y y y

z z z z z z

2　2　2　2　2　2　2　2　2　　　　3　3　3　3　3　3　3　3

4   4   4   4   4   4   4   5   5   5   5   5   5   5   5

6　6　6　6　6　6　6　6

7　7　7　7　7　7　7

8 8 8 8 8 8 8 8

9 9 9 9 9 9 9 9

o o o o o o o o o

The following pages show simple layouts which can be used for letters and envelopes, recipes, diaries, cards and so on. Stick to these suggestions at first, but later on you should experiment with layouts of your own.

For posters on a larger scale you will need to get much larger pens, called poster pens and witch pens. To avoid wasting paper, pencil in the words very lightly first, and write freely over the top. Never use more than three sizes of pen on the same page, or three colours. Black on its own may provide all the contrast you need.

All you need for this book is one cheap italic pen, medium italic size, and scrap writing paper. Ordinary ink will serve, but black is best.

Achnasheen, Braid Road, Auchterderran, Perthshire
12 · 12 · 96

Dear Morag

It was lovely to hear from you again, and to know that you will be home for Christmas! Do phone as soon as you land, and we can arrange to meet. We hope you can spend at least part of Christmas with us.

Duncan is staying with us over the holidays, so you'll see him too.

The children are delighted with the presents, and of course are longing to see you.

Love from all!

Anne

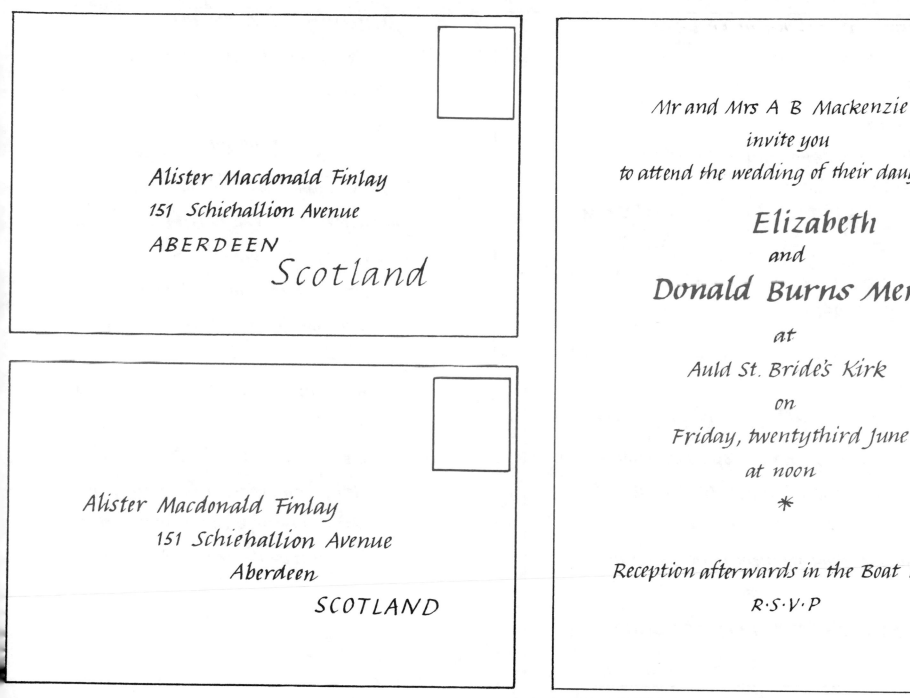

Alister Macdonald Finlay
151 Schiehallion Avenue
ABERDEEN
Scotland

Alister Macdonald Finlay
151 Schiehallion Avenue
Aberdeen
SCOTLAND

Mr and Mrs A B Mackenzie
invite you
to attend the wedding of their daughter

Elizabeth
and
Donald Burns Menzies

at
Auld St. Bride's Kirk
on
Friday, twentythird June
at noon
*

Reception afterwards in the Boat Hotel
R·S·V·P

```
           *
       *—*—*
     —*—*—*—
    —*—*—*—*—        Merry
   —*—*—*—*—          Christmas
       ═              and
       ═              a
                      Happy
       from           New
   Mac and Moira           Year!
```

Mary & John Cameron
invite you to attend the opening of their new
Gallery in the High Street, Dunaber, by
Sir Neil Macleod
on Saturday 12 June,   at 2.30 pm
*
Paintings · Pottery · Prints · Sculpture
*

January 3 : Menton

Walked to Roquebrune in the morning after
handing my bike in for repairs. Very cold, but
did a passable watercolour. The village is built
on a conglomerate rock, and where it's hewn to
make a path, looks like built rubble.

January 4 : Castellar

In spite of the dull weather, cycled up to
Castellar, finding the clouds nearer and nearer
all the way. Rain prevented sketching.

January 5 : Monaco

Found the famous Aquarium closed, so
went on to visit the old fort. Later I found
the coast road at Monte Carlo was being
deluged with spray from the heavy seas.
After my visit to Cap Martin, I decided
to return by the shorter Route Nationale.

Oatmeal Biscuits

10 oz oatmeal : 10 oz flour; 4oz butter:
4oz sugar : 1 egg : 1 teaspoon baking soda :
milk : salt .

RUB the butter into the oatmeal and the
flour. Add the sugar, baking soda and
salt. Beat the egg and add with enough
milk to make a stiff dough. Roll out thinly
and cut into rounds. Bake until crisp
in a moderate oven.

Blackcurrant Jam

4lbs blackcurrants : 8lbs sugar : 8 cups

ROMAN capitals, ancestor of all these scripts, and itself the flower of thousands of years development

uncial
Many early books were written in uncial scripts

quam — 5th century Roman

ȝehab — 8th century Irish

ERGO — 7th century English

round hand
The model for most of our modern type faces

omnium — 8th century Carolingian

miseran — 15th century Humanistic

script — 20th century [Edward Johnston]

black letter
Decorative, but illegible in many of its varieties

lapidem — 15th century French

aluares — 15th century Spanish

baptiza — 15th century Gothic

italic
Now adopted by many people as everyday writing

dirimpetto — 18th century Italian

questa parte — 16th century Italian

hombre — 16th century Spanish

How to make your own pens!

Bamboo, reed, almost any kind of pencil-sized twig can be made into a usable pen. They can be used green, but for a long lasting pen they are best seasoned for six months or more in a dry place.

The hollow bamboo or reed is best, but solid twigs are almost as good. Quills are not quite so easy to prepare, and are best avoided at this stage.

If you find it difficult to cut a straight slice as in ①, do it roughly, then rub down smooth and straight on fine sandpaper, stuck down on a flat surface. This method can also be used to finish the writing edge of the tip.

slice off end

split with a sharp knife

trim to desired width

nick off open tip with knife, on a

hard surface: approx. angle as here

ink reservoir - stiff tinfoil

2 m/m from tip   inside if hollow

tape outside if solid

if left-handed, cut at this angle

a

These are some of the materials which can be used to make pens. The harder ones may last for years. The very soft, like the strip of card used to write the "a" above, may only serve for one poster. Bamboo and reed are most durable, but all can be re-sharpened and used again, until too short to hold.

Bamboo *bamboo*

Raspberry

willow

reed elder

Making large poster pens

Here are two ways of making pens to any size you choose. For lettering six inches high, the width of the tip would have to be around one inch.

A slip of almost any straight grained wood will do. Not too thick, and not too thin and flexible; say two m/m.

The tip, cut or sandpapered, should be flat and straight, so ALL its width is in contact with the writing surface.

Note that the thin stroke of the felt pen will depend on the thickness of the felt.

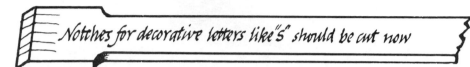

First make 5 or 6 splits at the end. Then cut or sandpaper

Notches for decorative letters like "S" should be cut now the tip at a sharp angle, and trim handle to a convenient width.

stiff tinfoil

Tape the tinfoil reservoir 1 m/m short of writing edge.

felt tin dowel rod

Felt pen assembled. Panel pins may be used for extra security.

Guide lines are permissible for the learner,
to help keep the body of the script an even
height, with its ascenders and descenders.

As you become more skilled, all guide lines
except the base line may be discarded. This
permits a more lively appearance than script
written between "tramlines", which tend to look
as though they were in a strait jacket.

Many scribes of old preferred to write BETWEEN
the lines, which were scored into the surface
of the vellum with a blunt point.

Lines may be dispensed with altogether by using
a thin writing paper placed over a template –
a sheet of paper with black lines already ruled
in. These will show through well enough to
serve as a guide.

Approximate guide lines: use half, one or two or more

Suitable for Mitchell's Round Hand pen Nº 1, or similar size